THE RULES UNRAVEL

~UNTANGLING LIFE'S THREADS IN VERSE

KAVYA MALIK

To my dearest friends, for the laughter, the tears, and the unwavering

support. This one's for you."

Contents

Foreword

Open this book, and you step inside a kaleidoscope of emotions. Here, joy dances with sorrow, laughter mingles with tears, and the quiet hum of contentment shares space with the fiery intensity of passion. These poems are an invitation to explore the rich tapestry of human feeling, in all its beautiful complexity. Within these pages, you'll find verses that resonate with your own experiences. Perhaps you'll relive the thrill of first love, the sting of betrayal, the quiet comfort of friendship, or the bittersweet pang of loss. These poems aim not to prescribe emotions, but to reflect them back, offering validation and a space for recognition. Whether you're seeking solace, understanding, or simply a deeper connection to your own inner world, let these poems be your guide. Dive into the depths of joy, navigate the storms of anger and grief, and allow yourself to be swept away by the currents of the human heart. Prepare to be surprised, challenged, and ultimately, moved.

Preface

This book is a peek into the world of feelings. We all experience happiness, sadness, anger, and everything in between. These poems are like little snapshots of those emotions.Some poems might make you smile, while others might make you feel a little teary. But that's okay! Emotions are a big part of who we are, and this book is a way to explore them together.So, dive in and see if you find a feeling you recognize. You might even discover a new one!

Acknowledgements

This book wouldn't exist without the incredible support system that carried me through this journey. First and foremost, my deepest gratitude goes to my family and teachers who supported and encourage me all the time by giving me advices and giving me their precious time. Their honest feedback pushed me to become a better writer and their enthusiasm kept me motivated always.

1. Emotions

Sunlight on my face,
Happiness in every space.
Tears like rain,
Headache's heavy chain.
Shadow in the night,
Trembling at the sight.

2. Rules of Happiness.

Everything gonna fall on place,
Travel the world and listen to others,
Don't give chance to society.
Keep shining, happiness doesn't last's,
Go overseas and love the life.
When you are young,
Follow your heart overheads.
Be wild, show some interest,
Are short lived happy,
In your skin and,
Make your own identity.

3. Empowered Passion

Standing tall in the face of challenges,

confidence unveils itself as a powerful force.

It dispels fear and empowers individuals to embrace their true potential.

In the fiery embrace of passion,

two hearts ignite a dance that burns with intensity.

It's a flame that fuels desire and forges connections.

4. Fear like a thread

Fear like a skilled weaver,
entwines our thoughts in a maze of doubts.
Its threads, though intangible, create a tangible sense of,
Unease challenging the bravest of hearts.
Fear like a skilled weaver entwines,
our thoughts in a maze of doubts.
Its threads, though intangible,
create a tangible sense of unease, challenging the bravest of hearts.

5. A faded Photograph

The edges blur,

the colors dim,

A smile that used to warm within.

Laughter's echo,

faint and thin,

A memory trapped where it's been.

Empty chair and a vacant space,

Haunted by a missing face.

Time is a thief,

leaves no trace,

Just a photograph's sad embrace.

6. Life

Tears never dry,
Memories never lie.
Heartbeats in tune,
Adventure under the moon.
Green-eyed stare,
Envy's poisonous snare.
Peaceful and still,
Serenity's gentle thrill.

7. Is that Okay?

Can someone stop time for a moment,
I feel like something is wrong,
I tried not to cry but,
Now I am sorry, I treated myself like that,
Don't tell me that's okay.
I dunno what ton do without you in these lonely days,
I wish I could have you together and forever always.

8. Why?

The words flow out,
My blood on a page
I will just sit here,
Drowning in a rage.
A small glass of bottle full of tears,
That I have held back ,
For thirteen years.
Why?
Why did I do?
To earn such a woe.
Why must I ?
Hate everything so.

9. Farewell

There is no love without farewell.
no love without farewell.
as likes kites rise up higher,
when wind blows stronger.
as bigger farewell brings,
more unbearable sorrow.
the deeper the love,
the bigger,
the grief.

10. Kindness

Holding the door,
for someone small Listening close,
when tears may fall.
Picking up trash for a cleaner ground,
Kindness is magic all around.
Little things done with care and thought,
Making the world, a nicer spot.
Be kind today, it's easy to see,
Kindness starts with you, and with me!

11. Reaching for More

Heart open wide,
Love's endless tide.
Darkness all around,
Lost, not found.
Bliss in every breath,
Life without death.
Aching for more,
Yearning at the core.
Walls closing in,
Patience wearing thin.
Goals finally met,
No room for regret.

12. Non-Fiction

Feel it cutting into me
The doubting painful knife,
Feel it depending the rift,
Finally hit just right.
Couldn't take the love,
I had so weak,
Burning low but it grew into a weapon only hurting me
This I know is non- fiction.
So good with number science, Math I like but I am terrible at English
so
I despite this part of me
That wants a simple
"Right and wrong"
And I always feel that I am always false
Can you even solve this problem?
Can you even stop the rope from hanging by neck?
Hey! Just tell me now
It's not like that i care now.

13. Thank You

Sun warms my face, a gentle breeze,
Rustling leaves in the tall green trees.
Birds sing a song, so sweet and clear,
Thankful for sounds I love to hear.
Family near with hugs so tight,
Smiling faces filling my sight.
Friends who play and make me laugh,
Thankful for joy that cuts in half,
Little things too, I won't forget,
Tiny ladybug, I haven't met.
Sparkling rain and a cozy nook,
Thankful for life, in every book